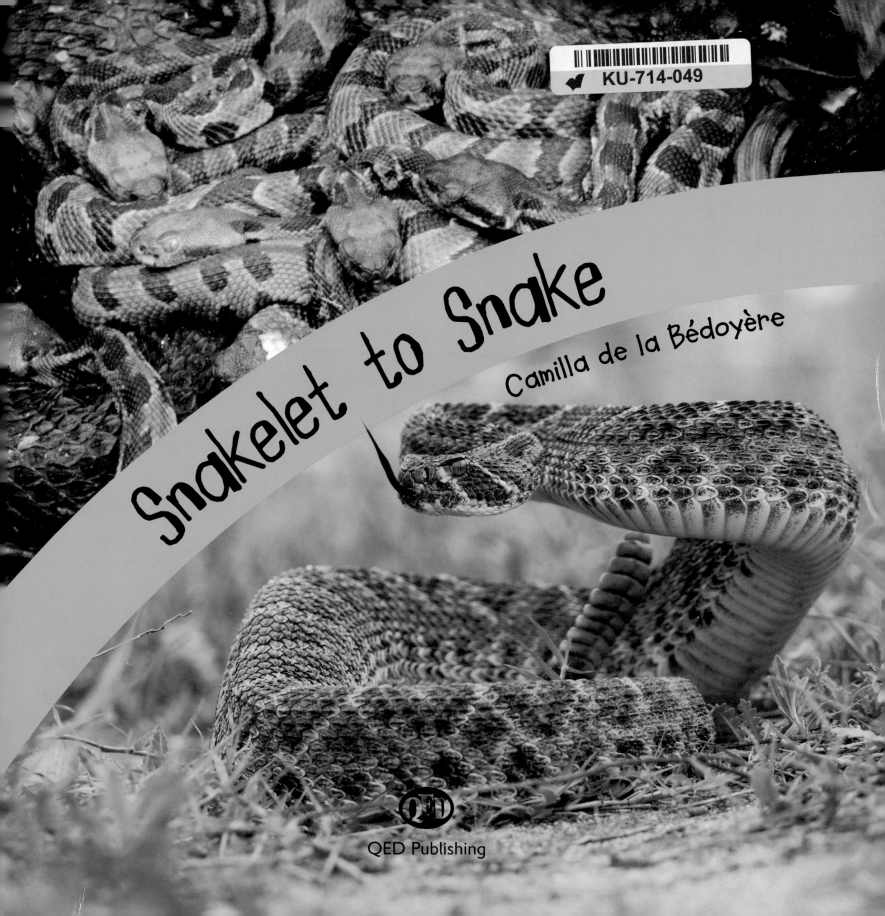

Snakelet to Snake

Camilla de la Bédoyère

QED Publishing

Words in **bold** are explained in the Glossary on page 22.

Editor Alexandra Koken
Designer and Picture Researcher Melissa Alaverdy

Contents

What is a snake?

A snake is a kind of **reptile**. Reptiles have **scales** on their skin. Most reptiles live on land and lay eggs.

Snakes do not have legs or eyelids. They move by slithering. They hunt other animals to eat. The animals they hunt are called **prey**.

⇨ Snakes cannot walk. Instead they slither.

scales

Crocodiles, lizards and turtles are also reptiles.

⇧ This lizard has spines on its back. It is a reptile.

⇦ Turtles are reptiles that live in the sea or rivers.

The story of a snake

Baby snakes are called **snakelets**. Most mother snakes lay eggs, but some give birth to snakelets.

Snakelets look like their parents, and quickly grow. Soon, they are old enough to become parents themselves.

⇒ These mother snakes have snakelets growing inside them. The mothers are pregnant.

snakelet

2

⇧ Newborn snakelets soon slither away from their mother.

1

mother

3

The amazing story of how a snakelet grows into an adult snake is called a **life cycle**.

adult snake

⇐ This snake is about 1 metre long.

The story begins

Male and female snakes come together to **mate**.

They find each other by smell. Snakes have a good sense of smell and they can smell things that are far away.

Most animals smell things with their nose, but snakes use their tongue.

tongue

⇧ When a snake flicks its tongue, it is smelling the air.

A female snake has eggs inside her body. When the snakes mate, the male **fertilizes** her eggs.

⬆ Some male and female snakes stay together for two days at mating time.

Laying eggs

The mother snake lays her fertilized eggs. A group of eggs is called a **clutch**.

Most snakes do not look after their eggs.

However, some snakes build nests for their eggs. They lie on the eggs to keep them warm. Warm eggs hatch sooner than cool ones.

⇧ Corn snakes lay their eggs and then slither away. Ten weeks later, the eggs hatch.

⇧ Burmese snakelets grow inside the eggs for two months. Their mother keeps them warm.

It can take many months for the snakelets to grow big enough to hatch.

A snakelet uses its **egg-tooth** to break out of the strong shell.

13

Giving birth

Some snakes do not lay eggs.
Instead the snakelets grow
inside the mother's body.

The snakelets are warm and safe
inside the mother's body. They
are safe from other animals that
want to eat them.

When the snakelets have grown,
the mother gives birth. Each
snakelet is tiny,
but it can look
after itself.

⇧ When a snakelet is
born it is covered in a
thin, see-through skin
called a membrane.

⇦ Adders give birth
to snakelets.

3

⇦ Newborn snakelets flick their tongues and look for food straight away.

Growing and moulting

As a snakelet grows, it loses its skin. This is called **moulting**. New skin has grown under the old skin.

A snake is an adult when it is about two years old.

It takes longer for big snakes to become adults. Snakes grow and moult all their lives.

Anacondas can grow for many years.

old skin

1 The old skin is dry. It splits at the head.

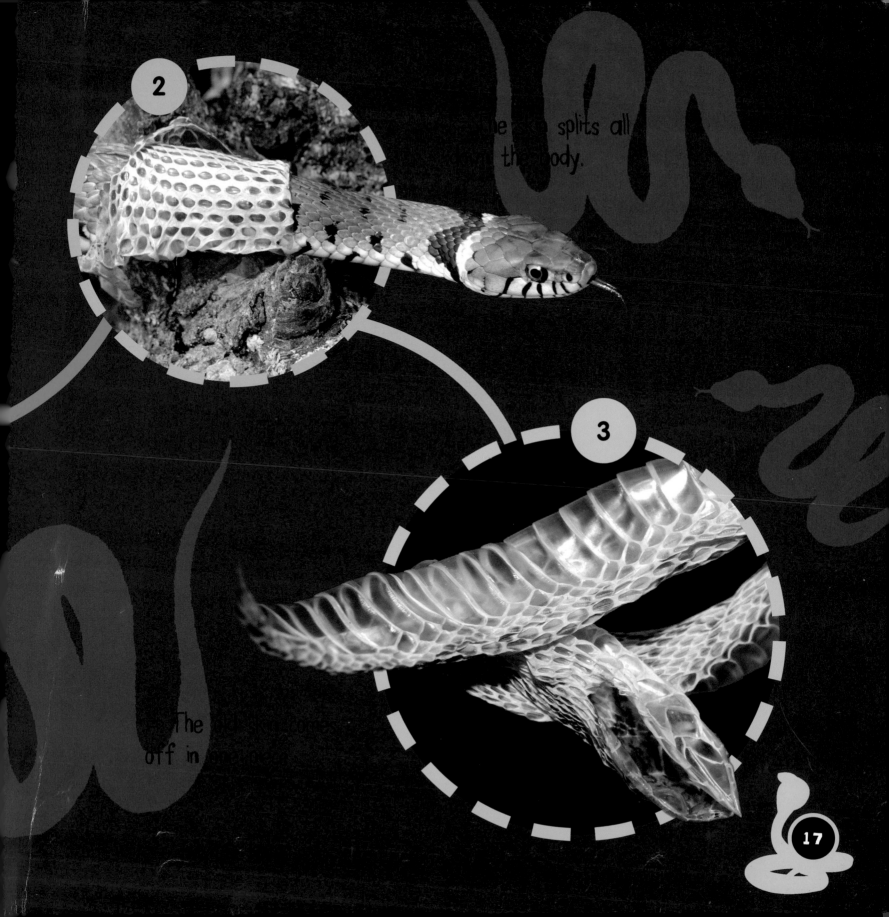

2 The skin splits all ~~down~~ the body.

The old ~~skin~~ comes off in ~~one piece~~.

3

17

Hunting

Snakes and snakelets hunt other animals to eat.

Snakes have sharp **fangs** in their mouth. Some fangs have **venom** in them. This is a poison that can kill small animals.

Snakelets hunt small animals, such as beetles.

fangs

⇦ Snakes are fast and fierce hunters.

18

Some big snakes hold other animals in their coils. They squeeze them to death.

⇧ Corn snakes hunt mice. They kill the mice in their coils.

Where snakes live

Most snakes live on the ground and in trees.

Snakes like to stay warm. When they are warm they can move quickly to catch prey. Snakes that live in warm places can mate all year.

⇨ Green snakes can hide in trees. They stay still, looking for food.

Snakes that live in cool places sleep through the winter. In spring, they wake up and mate. The life cycle begins again.

⇧ Some snakes are difficult to see. Their colours and patterns help them to hide.

Glossary

Clutch
A group of eggs.

Egg-tooth
A sharp tooth used by a snakelet to break out of its egg.

Fang
A sharp tooth.

Fertilize
When a male fertilizes a female's egg it can grow into a new living thing.

Life cycle
The story of how a living thing grows from birth to death and how it produces young.

Mate
When a male fertilizes the female's eggs the snakes are said to be mating.

Moulting
When a snake loses its old skin it is moulting.

Prey
Animals that are hunted for food are prey.

Reptile
An animal with scaly skin.

Scales
Small, thin, dry pieces of skin that cover a snake's body.

Snakelet
A baby snake.

Venom
A type of poison.

Index

Notes for parents and teachers

- Look through the book and talk about the pictures. Read the captions and ask questions about the things in the photographs that have not been mentioned in the text.

- Use the Internet*, or books, to find out about the life cycles of crocodiles and turtles. Use a map and the Internet to reveal the amazing journey that leatherback turtles undertake to complete their life cycle.

- Draw a poster together to show a snake's life cycle. The snake's body could be a collage of shapes cut from coloured paper, to show the scales and patterns.

- Reptiles, such as snakes, are popular attractions at zoos and wildlife parks. If possible, visit a reptile house so children can see snakes and watch how they live. Draw attention to their different sizes, patterns and colours. Discover how some snakes are camouflaged, but others are brightly coloured to warn other animals.

- Be prepared for questions about human life cycles. There are plenty of books for this age group that can help you give age-appropriate explanations.

*The publishers cannot accept responsibility for information, links, or any other content of Internet sites or third party websites.